# LA CANNE ROYALE

# La Canne Royale

## Two Nineteenth Century Treatises for La Canne de Combat

Larribeau "*Nouvelle Théorie du Jeu de la Canne*" (1856)

Humé and Renkin "*Traité et Théorie de Canne Royale*" (1862)

translated Chris Slee

**La Canne Royale**

Copyright © 2016 Chris Slee (translator)

ISBN: 978-0-9943590-3-2 (eBook)

ISBN: 978-0-9943590-2-5 (Print)

All Rights Reserved. No part of this publication may be reproduced, stored in a retrieval system, or transmitted, in any form or by any means – by electronic, mechanical, photocopying, recording or otherwise – without prior written permission from the copyright owner(s).

*Nouvelle Théorie du Jeu de la Canne,* by M. Larribeau. *Traité et Théorie de Canne Royale* by Eugène Humé and J. Renkin. It is asserted both these books are in the public domain.

Created at PressBooks.com for LongEdge Press. First edition.

La Canne Royale © Chris Slee. All Rights Reserved, except where otherwise noted.

*To Kathi and Henry,
Charlotte and Marianne*

# Contents

| | |
|---|---:|
| Introduction | 1 |

## New Theory of the Art of the Canne

| | |
|---|---:|
| Guide to Canne-Play | 7 |
| Foreword | 9 |
| First Part | 11 |
| Second Part | 23 |
| Post-Face | 43 |
| Figures | 45 |

## Treatise and Theory of the Canne Royale

| | |
|---|---:|
| Introduction | 77 |
| The Assault - The Bout - The Manner to Comport Oneself | 85 |
| Figures | 91 |

# Introduction

The two books presented in this volume, Larribeau's "New Theory" and Hume and Renkin's "Treatise and Theory," represent French stick fighting around the middle of the nineteenth century. They show how stick fighting was thought of and taught before the innovation and formalising of the discipline by Pierre Vigny at the end of the century, and its further incorporation into the Bartitsu of Edward Barton-Wright, and the modern sport largely developed by Maurice Sarry in the 1970s. Both books attempt to stand with a foot in each of the camps of practical self-defence and gymnastic exercise.

Self-defence was a necessity in the larger European cities and in Paris in particular by all accounts in the nineteenth century. Various methods of self-defence were promoted and popularised during the period ranging from boxing (whether *savate* or following the English style), canne or baton, two-handed baton, and fencing. Knives were the province of thugs and the criminal underclass and yet, while no person of quality would deign to carry one, some method of overcoming an attack made with a knife had to be found. Enter the walking stick or the canne. All successful gentlemen affected to carry a walking stick and an instructor claiming that, when properly trained, any man with one could fight off multiple opponents provided himself with a solid income.

The nineteenth century also saw a growing preoccupation with physical fitness. In the German and English-speaking spheres, this seems to have dwelt on strength and endurance with sport being conducive "not merely to physical, but to moral health."[1] In the French-speaking world, flexibility, balance and the ability to run, leap and climb appear to have been of at least equal importance. Both books, but more so Humé's, emphasise the health-giving aspects of the practice of canne-play, promoting both the purely physical benefits of vigour, strength and suppleness as well as the moral benefits of strength of character, self-assurance, and courage.

Late in the eighteenth century and at the beginning of the nineteenth century, the canne and the staff become something of the badge of office for several guilds and companies, most notably the stonecutters, carpenters, and lock makers. The symbols of their guilds were carved into to the wood and the wielder's rank within the guild was often evident in these symbols and codes. Some guild-masters and company trustees paid former soldiers and fencing masters

---

1. Saturday Review, 21 February 1857

to teach their apprentices how to use the staff and, increasingly, the canne for self-defence and the protection of the guild. By the middle of the nineteenth century, the canne was taught in the most exclusive clubs and fencing schools in France and it had largely lost its former poor reputation. By the last quarter of the century, it was compulsory to study the weapon at both the Joinville academy, in a military context, and in most public schools, as part of the physical education program. *La Canne* was presented as a demonstration sport at the Olympic Games of 1900 at Paris and enjoyed a considerable vogue until the start around of the First World War. It was during this time that Pierre Vigny, a confederate of Edward Barton-Wright, the creator of Bartitsu, produced his remarkable formulation of the art. It fell into disuse after the war until Maurice Sarry published his method of canne fighting as a sport in the 1970s.

There are small differences between the methods of canne-play taught in each book. For example, while both use a concept of striking to the "four faces" (in front, to the right, behind, to the left), Larribeau's four are enumerated in an anti-clockwise direction from the front whereas Humé's four faces are enumerated in a clockwise direction starting on the fencer's right-hand side. Larribeau's system teaching striking the four faces in a cross pattern, striking first at 1 and 3 then 2 and 4. Humé works consistently from one face to the next in a clockwise direction. Obviously, the concept of fencing to the four faces is an important one in the tradition of French stick fighting but, at this time, no single method of its implementation had gained universal acceptance.

The canne itself is different in each book. Larribeau boasts that he patented his canne although this cannot be confirmed at this time. However, the image on the frontispiece of his book shows two styles of canne, one with a round pommel, the other with a half-hook or handle, both having a wrist strap. It can be assumed to be of the same length as a standard walking stick, approximately one metre or a little less. Humé's canne is also not described. However, given that Humé refers to it specifically as "la canne royale," it is not a huge leap of the imagination to assume that it is the length of the standard measurement under the *Ancien Régime* of the same name, approximately 1.25 metres in length.

## The Authors

Larribeau, first name unknown, proudly proclaims on the title page of his book that he is one of the last survivors of the wreck of the *Meduse*, a French frigate which ran aground and sank off the coast of Africa in 1816. Of the 400 people on board, there was only space for 250 in the ships boats. All but a handful of the remaining 150 boarded a hastily-built raft and were set adrift with only one bag of ship's biscuit and two casks of water. When the raft was found by accident some two weeks later, only 15 men remained and tales of murder and cannibalism soon circulated. Blame for the incident was placed firmly at the feet of King Louis XVIII, newly restored to the throne after the defeat of Napoleon at Waterloo, and his appointment of an incompetent captain. Public outrage at the event cannot be underestimated. Larribeau is known to have taught a variety of martial arts including *la canne* and *savate*, French boxing.

Other than the book was published in Brussels, nothing in known about either Eugène Humé or T. Renkin. Both claim to be members of several fencing and boxing clubs but their name is not found in any of the directories of the fencing world such as Tavernier's <u>Amateurs et Salles d'Armes de Paris</u> (1886) or Goudourville's <u>Escrimeurs Contemporains</u> (1899).

## Translator's Notes

Technical terms have been for the most part rendered into English to make them understandable. The few terms which remain in French are either too unwieldy in translation to be readable or their meaning is clear and immediately intelligible to most people. Humé's book provides little difficulty in translation whereas Larribeau's use of semi-colons for periods, as well as for their proper use, leads to some educated guess work to determine where sentences end.

The French verb *prendre* (to take) has been translated as "make" in most cases to conform with modern English usage, eg: "make a face strike" and "the parry having been made" instead of the more literal "take a face strike" and "the parry having been taken."

The terms *volté* and *volté-face* appear regularly in the text. The first has not been translated as it is a term familiar to anyone with even a little fencing or HEMA experience. The second term has been translated as "about-face" as this seems to make better sense in context.

Larribeau at times fails to call out clearly whether he is talking about, for example, the fencer's right-hand side or the opponent's right-hand side. It is however always obvious when stepping through the action.

Other translation difficulties and the original French text are noted in footnotes throughout the text.

Original tables of contents have not been translated and are not included in this volume.

# New Theory of the Art of the Canne

Decorated with 60 figures[1] indicating the poses and the strikes by

M. Larribeau

Professor of fencing, canne and French boxing and of a special system of defence that he demonstrates in 10 lessons with the aid of the canne which he has patented[2]

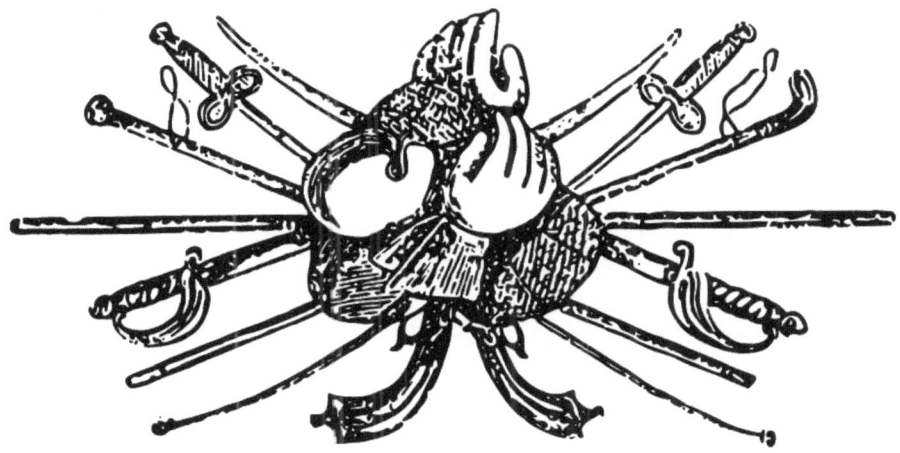

Prix: 9 francs

Paris

Chez l'Auteur, No.13 bis Passage Verdeau

---

1. Although there are only 42 figures illustrating the combat system
2. *pour laquelle il est breveté*

# Guide to Canne-Play

*Larribeau*

Professor for 40 years. Seaman for 20 years.

Present at the Battle of Trafalgar (23 October 1805) and one of the last survivors of the wreck of the *Medusa*.

18 bis Passage Verdeau at Paris, 1856

## Important Observation

Our system of personal defence, demonstrated in ten lessons, is completely independent of the general teaching developed in the theory of canne-play[1] that we have published. Its principal movements alone have been given[2] but together, the system properly called, we repeat, is foreign to this theory.

Through our system in ten lessons, we simplified canne-play, whose teaching requires longer study. We have done more: in order to arrive at the reality of personal defence, we invented a canne for which we have taken the patent.

---

1. *le jeu de la canne*
2. *puisés*

# Foreword

Fencing has always played a large role in education. It was in other times a necessary complement, if not the primary element. This is understandable. The sword formed then an integral part of the attire. In the town, at the ball, at court, one was never separated from it. In paging through ancient memoirs, we can understand the influence of this fashion on the mores of this period. One finds there, in this respect, incidents as curious as [they are] interesting.

But little by little habits [and] mores changed and the habitual carrying of the sword fell away.

After fencing lost its necessary character, it returned in the ornamental arts,[1] gymnastic exercise. We considered it above all as an auxiliary program for grace and bodily strength.

We will not examine it here, since it would not be indispensable to know fencing, from which derives all the other defensive arms, and of which in serious circumstances one can miss the knowledge.[2]

The sword is no longer carried, the fashion is now[3] the canne, a stick of *pomme d'or*[4] or varnished modest wood. It is in everyone's hands.

However, it is not only for poise that it has been adopted, it is also as a means of defense. Experience teaches that it could frequently render great service, that it was a redoubtable weapon in the hands of him who knew how to use it.

We add that the handling of the canne returned essentially in gymnastic exercises and that it should not only be seen in relation to the development of muscular strength, but one should also consider the suppleness, the agility that it gives them. From there, to elegance, to grace in movement, it is not far.

Canne-play, in order to use the practical term, is therefore of a real importance, and a treatise which teaches it methodically, theoretically, cannot fail[5] to be as useful as interesting.

It is this work that we have undertaken: the result of long studies and of more than forty years of theory and practice. Clarity and precision were our aims. We hope to have achieved them. We wanted that a thoroughly indiffer-

1. *les arts d'agrément*
2. *on peut regretter la science*
3. *inauguré*
4. the exact meaning is unclear
5. *ne peut manquer*

ent man,[6] even with the most simple notions of fencing, could grasp and understand the details into which we enter that by their study he could [by] himself, without needing a master, learn to defend himself with the aid of the canne against unforeseen attack.

In order to give more precision to our demonstrations, we have accompanied them with figures explaining the poses, the strikes indicated, with cross-reference notes[7] in the text.

We have the conviction, without wanting to injure any[one's] pride, that is far from our thoughts, without claiming to belittle any[one's] deserved merit, that would be beneath us, of being useful to many teachers, in the true connotation[8] of the word, who have the title of teacher, of whom pure routine[9] is the only guide, and who have no notion of demonstrative theory. It does not suffice however to know the weapons in order to teach them. Yet he should know also [how] to demonstrate them clearly, precisely. Practice and theory are two distinct domains,[10] and practice and theory reunited make a good master since a good master can alone train a good student.

Our method, which allows us to teach the canne in ten lessons, gives us the right to claim the title as well as to guarantee the result. Besides, experience has adjudged on this double claim.

The reader will now adjudge on the theory.

6. *tout homme étranger*
7. *notes de renvois*
8. *acception*
9. tradition?
10. *sciences*

# First Part

### 1st – The Necessary Tools

Before any explanation, we must understand the primary materials with which the student must be furnished in order to learn the moves of the canne.

He should have:

- A glove with a sleeve[1] of hide or varnished leather,
- An arm guard filled with horsehair,
- A mask with a metal grill,[2]
- A belt to ensure the sturdiness of the kidneys,
- Suitable footwear, as much as possible slippers in soft leather in order to avoid any inconvenience to movement.

Thus for the student. We pass now to a utensil which regards exclusively to the master.

Guided by our long experience in teaching the exercise of our own body in personal defence, we adopted, in order to exercise our students in the different movements that they have to execute, a pad or mannequin for which here is the description and the form.

It seems to us indispensable in an exercise hall.

This pad consists of a strong platform of oak covered in hide or in thick canvas if needed, stuffed with horsehair or oakam, to form a well-rounded back and to furnish two strong hooks[3] convenient for the exercise room.

It has a long form (1 metre 30 centimetres in length) and carries in its upper part 40 centimetres of width in order to have no more, by successive and imperceptible narrowing, than 30 centimetres of width in the lower part. (See plate no.1)

We created this mannequin not only with the aim of facilitating students in the study of the handling of the canne in the different movements and strikes which it calls for,[4] but also in order to teach the first principles of French boxing. We will add therefore that our pad is furnished inside with springs which

---

1. *crispin*
2. *toile metallique*
3. *crampons*
4. *qu'il exige*

give it the necessary elasticity to give way and return under the pressure of the kicks and punches that the student makes while exercising.

Some words on the usefulness of this tool: it allows the student to exercise himself without fear and develop by consequence the agility and rapidity of these movements. We recognised, in our long practice, that it is always the cause of nearly instantaneous progress. We cannot forget that it is a great help for the teacher besides. This last,[5] in effect, can, while one or two students exercises themselves on the pad, give a lesson to a third. He has only to throw a simple glance in order to correct false movements or false strikes.

With the pad, no time is lost for either the student or the teacher. (See plate no.5)

## 2 – Guiding the step and the retreat

In order to direct the student in the study of the step and the retreat, here is our method:

We arrange along the length of the exercise room, in a straight line consequently, a course that we mark by points hereafter indicated, separating them by an interval of around 50 centimeters.

The two tracks drawn above A to 2, and below 1 to 3, from B to 8 above, from 9 to 7 below are explained by the examples following.

It may be:

$$\overbrace{A. \underbrace{1. 2}\ 3. 4.}\ 5.\ 6.\ \overbrace{7. 8. 9. B.}$$

*Example*: Being in true guard, that is to say, the left foot on point A and the right foot on point 1, in order to advance, carry the left foot from A to 2, as the track indicates from point A to point 2. Having fallen into false guard, in order to continue his step and retake true guard, advance the right foot and carry this foot from point 1 to point 3, following the indication of the track 1 to 3.

These explanations govern all the steps until the point given as B.

It's a matter now of beating the retreat.

*Example*: Being found in true guard [with] the right foot on B, the left on 9, in order to effect the retreat movement, carry first the right foot from B to 8, then the left foot from 9 to 7, as indicated by the two tracks leading from B to 8 and 9 to 7.

---

5. ie: the instructor

Thus, the milestones which can guide the student in the progression of the straight line. We will indicate, when we come to the progression of the about-face, the arrangement of the indicative tracks to follow.

We pass now to the first elements of the handling of the canne.

## 3 – First Exercises of the Canne

### 1. Of the Right Guard and Position of the Body

Stand straight, upright, the canne in the right hand. Hold it by the big end, the hand passed through the cord which holds it, in a manner that it cannot escape in different movements, placing the left hand behind the kidneys, the elbow as close to the body as possible, in order to avoid being hit in the progressions of the canne. Advance a little the right hand to the height of the chest, the arm slightly shortened, the little end of the canne in front of the right eye, the hand inverted, the fingers downwards (in *tierce*, the fencing term). Close the two heels in a manner to form a square, the hamstrings tight, the head high looking directly ahead, the chest flat.

### 2. Of the True Guard

In order to find true guard, bend the two knees carrying the right foot forward a distance of 50 centimetres, from A to 1, the two heels on the same line, the body upright on the legs. (See plate no.1)

### 3. Of the False Guard

The movement is made as the preceding, but it is the left foot which is carried forward, the right arm a little more lengthened, the hand in the same position, the left shoulder facing directly to the front.

### 4. Of the Step and Retreat

We indicated already this double movement in understanding[6] the usefulness of our track. We revisit it here in order to better clarify and in order to follow the order of teaching.

Being in true guard, the left foot on A, the right foot on 1, carry the left foot forward from the right from A to 2, and the right foot forward from the left from 1 to 3, continuing thus these alternate movements until one has arrived at the extremity of the line to travel, or point B.

---

6. *en faisant connaitre*

The retreat is worked in the opposite direction. Thus, the right foot being on B and the left foot on 9, carry the right foot from B to 8 and the left from 9 to 7, falling into false guard.

### 5. Of Changing Guard

Being in true guard the left foot on 9, the right foot on B, in order to change guard without shifting place make a semi-turn[7] to the left by a pivot movement on their respective points and face towards point A.

### 6. Of the Step Without Changing Guard

Being in true guard, in order to advance without changing guard, carry in an almost simultaneous impulse the left foot on point 1 to the place occupied by the right foot, and the right foot to point 2.

The guard is always the same, the right foot in front of the left, making thus to face the extreme point B.

In order to make the retreat execute the same movements for the step but execute them backwards.

Thus, carry backward the right foot from B to 8 and the left foot from 9 to 7, and continue until the point of departure.

The movement of the step and retreat that we have just indicated serves in the attacks and the ripostes with which we will occupy ourselves later.

### 7. Simple Face Strikes in True Guard

(See plate no. 1 and 2 depicting the student and the pad)

Being in true guard, raise the hand above the head, the little end of the canne directed on the left, the hand inverted, the fingers turned upwards[8] to the left ear, describe next a horizontal angle with the canne, lengthening the arm of all its reach to go to hit the strike on the top of the pad (the face of the supposed adversary) the hand always inverted but the fingers downwards.

The strike made, retake immediately the true guard position, the body and the hand in the same position as previously.

Repeat frequently this strike on the pad in order to render it familiar.

### 8. Simple Face Strikes in False Guard

In order to develop the strike, lift the hand above the head in the direction to the right presenting the left side of the face to the pad. (See plate no.3)

---

7. *un demi-tour*

8. *les ongles en l'air tournés*

Next, make the canne describe a horizontal circle above the head, lengthening the reach of the arm, then withdraw the left shoulder to approach the right, invert the hand fingers in the air in order to hit.

We will see here at once and for all that one must never extend the thumb on the canne. One should, on the contrary, hold it in the full hand and make it roll between the first fingers and the thumb. This is the true means to obtain more ease with less fatigue in the movements of the wrist.

### 9. Double Face Strikes

Double face strikes are made with the same movements as the simple strikes.

Lift the hand following the same rules but describe the first turn above the head, without extending the arm to hit. The first turn is only destined to give more force to the second, after which one lengthens the arm and one hits the pad.

### 10. Face Strikes to the Left

Place oneself as one does for the simple face strike. Lift the hand to the right slightly inclining the body, roll the canne in the hand and make it describe a double horizontal turn above one's head, then extend the arm and hit.

### 11. Kidney Strikes

[There are] few words to say on these strikes. As with strikes to the stomach, the chest, on the legs, they differ in nothing from the movements of the face strikes to the right or to the left. It's a matter only of hitting higher or lower.[9]

### 12. Head Strikes

Place oneself in front of the pad, the body straight and upright, the legs straight, the heel of the left foot near the instep of the right foot,[10] the left hand behind the kidneys, the right hand inverted, the thumb above without extending it along the canne.

This position taken, invert the hand the fingers downwards in lifting it to the rear to the left, leaving the little end of the canne to slope in this direction (see plate no.5) then carry rapidly the canne forwards extending the arm to its full extent and hitting vigorously the head strike, as we have just said in the preceding paragraph.

---

9. literally, more or less low
10. *la boucle du pied droit*

From this position lift again the hand letting fall the little end of the canne to the right (see plate no.7) carrying it behind the kidneys. (see plate no.6)

We will repeat here that which we had occasion to say for the first movement. If one wants to learn well the head strike, one should re-iterate often this movement on the pad. One should finally always retain the right guard if one wants to easily get used to these two changes of strike from the right and the left.

### 13. Double Head Strikes

Place oneself in true guard in front of the pad. Lift the hand to the left as if to develop a leg strike or kidney strike. Extend the arm to its full extent, carrying the hand from low to high, from left to right, inverting it from *tierce* in order to bring it forward and above the head, the little end of the canne facing the pad. Then without stopping the movement let it fall to the left in order to carry it behind and thus hit a head strike.

Replace oneself immediately in true guard in order to repeat the same movement. (See plate no.5)

This strike needs to be studied in order to grasp the double movement. Once it is understood, it gives a great easiness to learning the other head strikes.

### 14. Head Strikes by Moulinet[11]

These strikes are part of our system of defence taught in ten lessons. They are one of the principal movements.

The *moulinet* is without parry.[12] A man well exercised in this movement, could without fear wait on firm feet for an aggressor, whomever he may be, were he armed with a canne stronger than his own. He can be certain that by the movement of the moulinet well executed, there where he would like to make the strike, he will not meet a parry. The strike will be received.

Here is the position to take.

Place oneself in false guard, the left shoulder facing the pad, the body covered[13] and inclined to the right, but looking forward, the hand lifted behind. In this position, roll the canne behind from low to high, as indicated by plate no.8.

We take always the movement of rotation from high to low on the left and from low to high on the right, because, in this position, one is equally able to hit either a head strike or a face strike.

---

11. *The circular movement of the canne in the vertical plane to either the left or right of the fencer*
12. *le moulinet est sans parade*
13. *effacé*

Thus, for the head strike, it is always at the moment that the canne rolls in the hand that one executes the movement on the pad.

One must exercise oneself often in the movement in order to well possess it.

### 15. Of the Pass Forwards

The pass forward is a movement in five steps for the head strike, which needs to be studied with care in order to be well understood. It is again part of our system of defence in 10 lessons.

Place oneself in true guard, the hand in *quarte*, the fingers in the air. Carry the hand to the left in order to develop a strong face strike to the right of the pad, without stopping the movement imparted to the canne. It must not hit but pass close by.[14] Carry immediately the foot and the hand backwards without changing face, looking always on the contrary at the pad, taking the first movement of the *moulinet* (from low to high) in order to extend the head strike forwards, letting the canne fall to the left, in order to gather it next from high to low to the right, the hand inverted, the fingers in the air, carrying the little end of the canne behind in order to gather it from high to low making it pass close to the chest from left to right.

Finally, bring back the hand behind in order to retake the *moulinet* movement which follows a strong head strike hit on the pad, advancing rapidly the right foot.

This strike is made pivoting on the left foot in order to make again the movement if one wants to not replace oneself into guard.

### 16. From Face to Face for the Point Strike in Two Hands

Place oneself in front of the pad, in the position of the guard on the left, the legs straight, as if one had an adversary before oneself, the little end of the canne in the left hand and right hand behind holding the large end (see plate no.41)

For making the strike by a feinting retreat,[15] quickly withdraw the two hands behind the large end of the canne, then hit briskly with the little end at the height of the lower stomach of the pad. In giving the strike, leap backwards with both feet in order to place oneself immediately in true guard in front of the pad.

---

14. *frôler*
15. *une feinte de retraite*

### 17. Point Strike at the Face with a Head Strike

Double the face strike to the right by describing a third turn of the canne above one's head, in order to bring the little end in front of the pad, the right hand placed on the chest, the elbow near the body and the left foot forward of the right. (See plate no. 28)

This position is only a threat of a strike, it is a feint. In order to hit the point strike at the face (see plate no.30) extend the arm to its full extent,[16] the hand in the same attitude, the fingers upwards, solely in order to well direct the end in a straight line, extending the thumb along the canne. As soon as the strike is given, follow it with a strong head strike, (see the track on plate no.30) carrying the right foot forward in order to fall into true guard. Finally, make the canne describe a circle to the left and bring it back thus to oneself, the little end to the height of the eye.

### 18. The Flying Point Strike

Being is true guard, develop a face strike to the left leaving the right foot forward. By a rapid movement grasp the canne in the middle with the left hand that one allows to slide immediately up to the little end. Raise then the left hand to the level of the left shoulder, inverting the fingers in the air and the thumb close to the little end of the canne, the right hand resting at the height of the chest. If necessary, one can in this attitude take the right guard.

This position constitutes the strike's feint. In order to execute the movement, (see plate no.36) extend the left arm to its full extent releasing the large end that the right hand held. (See plate no.37)

The strike made, carry immediately the left foot forward of the right, releasing the large end of the canne that one brings rapidly to the right in order to grasp it immediately with the right hand that one raises to the level of the forehead, directing at the same time forward to the right, the little end at the height of the lower abdomen in order to make the kidney parry.

Depending on the situation,[17] make the head parry by lifting both hands. (See plates no. 38 and 39)

The point strike could be followed at the same time with a head strike, making the canne pass from low to high in order to bring it forward, the large end grasped in the right hand.

---

16. *dans toute sa portée*
17. *suivant les circonstances*

## 19. The Point Strike in False Guard

Place oneself [with] the left hand on the chest, holding the little end of the canne. This hand must be inverted on the inside, the thumb at two centimeters from the little end, the right arm brought behind, the right hand at chest height, holding the large end of the canne. (See plate no.41)

In this position, one is in distance to stop an assailant by a strike with the little end, extending the left arm and closing the right arm to the left in order to give more force to the movement. One finds oneself finally in the parry with two hands and leaping backwards in riposte with a face strike. (See plate no.32 which indicates the position to take)

## 20. Parries and Ripostes to the Right

In order to protect[18] the face to the right, place oneself in right guard, the hand and the fingers outside to the right, extending the right arm carrying the hand a little to the right, the little end of the canne lightly inclined to the left in order to avoid the canne of your adversary, hitting yours, not coming to slide on your fingers. (See plate no.42)

This parry made, return a riposte to the left lifting the hand to the right and making the canne describe a horizontal circle above one's head, and hitting next a face strike to the left extending the arm to its full extent lunging[19] with the right foot. (See plate no.4)

This strike, being a parry on the left and a riposte on the left, one must recover[20] into right guard, if one does not want to expose oneself to being injured from the face to the legs.[21]

## 21. Parries and Ripostes to the Left

Place oneself in right guard, the hand and the fingers inverted on the inside, left the hand to the left ear, a little above the head, to develop a face strike to the right, and on the parry return a riposte to the left, lunging with the right foot.

One should not forget that each time that one makes a face strike, being in right guard, one must lunge in order to return a riposte and lift in order to take the parry.

The parries and ripostes from the right and from the left are very important. One should repeat them often in order to render them familiar.

---

18. *parer*
19. *en se fendant*
20. *se relever*
21. *si l'on ne veut s'exposer à être trompé de la figure aux jambes*

### 22. Kidney Parry[22]

The kidney parry is made against strikes carried to the right. (See plate no.20)

After having taken the parry, the arm extended, the hand at the height of the right shoulder, the fingers inverted on the outside, the little end of the canne below, lift the hand making the little end pass across one's left, describing a horizontal circle above one's head in order to return the riposte of the face strike to the left of the teacher, lunging with the right foot. Lift oneself immediately in order to take again the parry to one's right.

These movements are made in false guard. (See plates no. 20 and 30)

We again recommend practising them often.[23]

### 23. The Parry of the Stomach and the Chest

Having just explained the kidney parry, we pass to the demonstration of the stomach and chest strikes.

The guard being always [on the] right, bring the hand to the left, extending only a little the arm in front.

The stomach and the chest parry only allows the return of another simple riposte, either to the head or to the face, to the adversary's left. One can try nonetheless a feint to the head in order to return a face strike to the right.

Regarding the leg parry, we will not speak of it. The leg should only be parried by evasion or a leap to the rear in order to return a riposte either to the head or to the face, on the wrist, or by a point strike to the face.

### 24. The Parry and Riposte of the Head Strike

Being in the head parry in right guard, the arm extended, the hand inclined ahead to the right, the little end of the canne to the left, directed slightly forward. Allow the little end of the canne to fall carrying the hand to the left, and lunge swiftly to return the riposte of the head strike on the teacher, who makes to retake promptly the right position through a head riposte. (See plates no.9 and 10)

The same advice as previously [given]: one should exercise this movement often.

### 25. The Head Parry, the Hand in Quarte

This parry is most often made after a face strike or stomach strike to the adversary's left. In this movement, the position of the hand differs in nothing from

---

22. *la parade des reins*
23. *les renouveler souvent*

that which one takes in order to parry to one's left. One raises the right hand to the left, the little end of the canne directed to the right. (See plates no. 17 and 18)

The riposte of the head is caught by[24] the head parry, the hand in *quarte*.

It is of great usefulness, as we see it, for the riposte from the face strike, from the stomach strike, and from the leg strike. It asks to be studied and repeated frequently.

---

24. *faire prendre*

# Second Part

We just finished the first part of our work by exposing succinctly the strikes which constitute the parry and the riposte. We believe however it is useful to push the necessity of well understanding the flying point strike, or, to say better, the parry with two hands. This movement can appear a little difficult but, with study and practise, one cannot fail[1] to succeed to possess it, and, we repeat, it is useful, indispensable to know it.

We recommend equally to well exercise oneself in feints. It is an essential point in the handling of the canne. Moreover, their teaching is completely the responsibility of the teacher. It is to him that the advice is addressed most particularly.

We arrive now at the second part. It comprises the progressive demonstration, in thirty divisions, of all the strikes which are attached to the theory of canne-play.

At the head of each of these divisions, we have placed as the title a summary of their aim.

By means of this summary, students who are following these lessons, or who have been taught after our method, have no need to read the entirety of each division in order to put into practise the lesson which it contains. This summary will be an *aide-mémoire* absolutely sufficient for them.

Regarding persons foreign to the handling of the canne who will read this publication, we have the hope that they will grasp easily the whole of our method and that they will thus be able to make rapid progress in this exercise, as useful as it is beneficial.

## 1st Division

### Forward Step

Place oneself in true guard, lift the hand to develop a simple face strike to the right,[2] carrying the left foot forward from the right and falling into false guard, then lift the hand to the right in developing a strong simple face strike in front, and fall into true guard.

Continue these same movements until one arrives at the end of the salle.

---

1. *on ne peut manquer*
2. The opponent's right hand side

### Retreat

Place oneself in true guard, develop a face strike to the right, carrying the right foot backwards and falling into false guard.

Repeat these movements until one returns to the point of departure.

### Breakdown of these Movements

The track of the indicative points is:

## A. 1. 2. 3̄. 4. 5. 6. 7. 8. 9. B.

### Stepping Forward

The student is in true guard, the left foot on A, the right foot on 1, he wants to go forward.

He lifts the right hand, developing a simple face strike to the right, carrying the left foot from A to 2.

The face strike finished, he has fallen into false guard. In order to retake true guard and continue his march, he repeats the movement of the simple face strike developing it to the left and carrying the right foot from 1 to 3.

The succession of these movements follows to the end point B.

### Retreat

The student has arrived in true guard[3] at point B, the left foot on this point, the right foot on 9.

He develops a simple face strike to the left, carrying the left foot backwards from B to 8.

The strike finished, he has fallen into false guard.[4] In order to continue the retreat movement he, repeats the simple face strike developing it to the right and carrying the right foot from 9 to 7.

Alternately repeat these movements until the point of departure.

## 2nd Division

### The Same Movements of the Step and Retreat; Double Face Strikes

Develop a face strike, but instead of extending the arm at the first turn that the

---

3. read: false guard?
4. read: true guard?

canne describes above the head, make it describe a second, extending the arm in order to hit either to the left or to the right, following the guard.

This movement is executed either advancing or withdrawing.

## 3rd Division

*The Same Movements of Step and Retreat; Double Face Strikes with a Head Strike*

Being in true guard, lift the hand to the left doubling a strong face strike to the right, and carry the left foot forward from the right, from point A to point 2, stopping the canne on the right shoulder and letting it fall backwards, the hand very close to the shoulder lowering the elbow in order to have more force, and then hit a strong head strike on the teacher, who takes the parry.

Repeat the same strikes from point A to point B.

We pass to the movements to execute for the retreat.

Being in true guard, develop a double face strike carrying the right foot backwards from the left, then after having neared the canne on the right shoulder according to the principles indicated above, make a violent head strike bringing the left foot behind the right.

One only stops once returned to the point of departure A.

## 4th Division

*Double Face Strikes, Head Strike with Changing Face*

Being in true guard the left foot on point A, the right foot on point 1, develop a double face strike to the right advancing the left foot to point 2, bringing the canne to the right shoulder and without pausing hitting a head strike carrying the right foot to 3.

Repeat the first movement of the double face strike to the right, advance the left foot from point 2 to point 4, hitting the head strike and carrying the right foot from point 3 to point 5. Then leap forwards turning rapidly on oneself[5] and developing a double head strike and falling into true guard.

In order to execute this last movement remove[6] the left foot from point 4 to point 6 and bring the right foot behind the left.

We retake the same movements that we just made in order to finish at point A facing B.

---

5. *en tournant rapidement sur soi-même*

6. *détacher*

## 5th Division

*Double Face Strikes Backwards and Forwards*

Being in true guard, the left foot on A and the right on 1 develop a double face strike, first to the right facing B advancing rapidly the left foot on point 2, and the second to the right facing A (behind) by a sudden[7] movement to the side, but without moving the feet and falling into false guard. Next make again a double face strike, the first to the left facing A carrying swiftly the right foot from 1 to 3, the second to the left facing B repeating the sudden movement to the side and falling into true guard.

Continue thus until point B and in order to beat the retreat[8] until point A execute the same series of movements.

The development of strikes as movements of the body requires the greatest nimbleness.

## 6th Division

*Double Face Strikes with Head Strikes Backwards and Forwards*

Being in true guard, develop a double face strike, the first to the right facing B and carrying swiftly the right foot to point 2 and the second to the right facing A by a sudden movement to the side pivoting on the two heels and bringing the canne to the right shoulder, then without pausing hit the first head strike facing A, next make a new and prompt pivot movement, advancing the right foot to point 3, stretching a head strike falling into true guard.

Repeat thus these movements until point B, and retreat towards point A.

## 7th Division

*Double Face Strikes Forward and Backwards, Double Head Strikes Forwards and Backwards by an About-Face and Head Strike Broken to the Right*

Being in true guard develop a face strike, the first to the right facing B, the second facing A turning the body swiftly to the right without pausing in the movement of the canne and carrying the left foot behind to point 2, bringing the canne immediately to the right shoulder, making to face B pivoting rapidly on both heels and stretching[9] a double head strike, the first facing B carrying

---

7. *brusque*
8. *pour battre en retraite*
9. *allongéant*

the right foot forward by a leap from point 1 to point 3, the second facing A, advancing with a spring[10] turning the left foot on point 4, Without stopping, develop by a movement of rotation from low to high a face strike and face B pivoting rapidly on the left.

Make again a double head strike, the first facing B advancing the right foot from 3 to 5, the second facing A carrying swiftly by a prompt pivot movement stepping the left foot from 4 to 6 and falling into true guard facing A.

Repeat the about-face movement and the series of other strikes in order to arrive at point B.

## 8th Division

### *Double Face Strikes and Point Strike*

Being in true guard, the left foot on A, the right foot on 1, double a face strike to the right advancing the left foot to 2, the strike made (but not hit) make the canne describe a third turn above the head, bringing the little end facing before one, the right hand near the right breast, the elbow touching the body, (see plate no.28) stretching the arm to its full extent and hit a point strike either to the face or to the chest, then develop a head strike lunging the right foot crossing from number 1 to number 3.

For the retreat, repeat these movements.

## 9th Division

### *Double Face Strike, Point Strike Forward, Backwards with an About-Face and Head Strike*

Being in true guard, the left foot on A, the right foot on 1, double a face strike to the right advancing the left foot to 2. The strike made, make the canne describe a third turn above the head, bringing the little end before oneself, stretching the arm to its full extent and hitting the strike, then develop a head strike, lunging, the right foot crossing[11] from number 1 to number 3 and falling into true guard.

Make again these same movements in order to bring the left foot to point 4, the right on point 5 in true guard. Making to face B, develop then a face strike facing B, pivot rapidly on the heels to face A, and bring the little end before oneself, in the position previously indicated, lengthen the arm and hit, from the same time, extend a head strike, develop a face strike always facing A,

10. step? leap?
11. *franchissant*

and without time to stop, by a lively pivot movement, carry the left foot from point 4 to point 6 making to face B, then bring the canne to the right shoulder.

In this position develop a double face strike, the first facing B advancing the right foot from 5 to 7, and the second facing A carrying, by a lively pivot movement backwards, the left foot from point 6 to point 8, and making immediately an about-face in order to arrive at points 9 and B falling into false guard.

Make again the same series of movements in order to return to the point of departure A.

## 10th Division

*Development[12] in Two Times to the Right and in One Time to the Left by a Single Change of Guard*

Being in true guard, the body well clear, the canne placed on the left shoulder in the form of a necktie,[13] (see plate 34) the little end directed towards B, the elbow and the hand as close to the body as possible, develop a first face strike to the right facing B carrying rapidly the left foot to point 2, hitting the second strike facing A turning rapidly the head and the body from this side without moving place, make immediately to face B always in place stretching a third face strike and bring the canne to the left shoulder.

This movement finished, turn swiftly the head behind towards point A. Describe a first face strike across this point. Develop the second facing B advancing rapidly the right foot from 1 to 3, turning swiftly again the head towards A, hitting a third face strike and bring the canne to the left shoulder.

Continue thus with a single change of guard until point B. The same movement for the retreat.

## 11th Division

*Double Face Strikes Forward and Backwards or Development in Four Times*

Being in true guard, the canne on the left shoulder in the previous position, develop two double face strikes, the first facing B, the second facing A, pivot rapidly, the left foot advanced to point 2, then turn oneself quickly to face B, the canne brought on the right shoulder in the form of a necktie, the little end directed forward.

Make again this movement by two double face strikes, the first carried fac-

---

12. *évolution*
13. *en forme de cravate*

ing B, the second facing A, the right foot brought by the same pivot movement from point 1 to point 3, and make again to face to B.

Continue these movements until point B.

The same movements for the retreat.

## 12th Division

### *Development in Four Times [and] a Single Change of Guard*

Being in true guard, the canne carried on the left shoulder, develop a double face strike to the right facing B carrying rapidly and turning the left foot from A to 2, the right on 3 in order to hit a second face strike towards point A, and without pausing send again two face strikes in place from one shoulder to the other, the first to the left, the second to the right, and stop the canne on the right shoulder.

The four face strikes made, without interruption and counting one, two, three, four, make again the strikes indicated to the left carrying the right foot from 1 to 3 and travel thus the line of indicative signs from A to B, the same for the retreat towards point A.

## 13th Division

### *Development in Six Time with an About-Face, Double Head Strike Forwards, Backwards and Two Changes of Guard*

Being in true guard, execute the same movements indicated in the previous division, but hit six face strikes instead of the four counting one, two, three, four, five, six in order to mark the strike.

These six full strikes[14] done, being in false guard, the right foot on 1 and the left on 2 the canne on the right shoulder making to face B, make a rapid leap turning in order to fall by two changes of guard the right foot on 3 and the left on 4 facing A, and hit, making an about-face, a double head strike, the first towards B, in true guard, the second towards A in false guard.

Make again then the first movements, developing a double face strike towards the right, hitting the six strikes, stretching through two changes of guard with an about-face the double head strike, the one facing A, the other facing B, and continue thus until point B. Make to face A and repeat the same movements for the retreat.

---

14. *coups allongés*

## 14th Division

*Development in Three Times on the Four Faces by the Right*

Here we have recourse to another guide for the step. This is no longer a straight line, it is a square whose sides are 1, 2, 3, 4 and the middle O distant by a given interval of 80 centimetres.

Here is the figure:

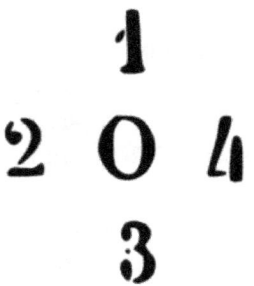

This guide indicated, we explain the movement.

Being in true guard, the left foot on 1, the right foot on O facing 3, the canne brought to the left shoulder (see plate 34 for the pose) develop a double face strike, the first facing 3, the second to the right towards 4, without pausing and from the same impulse of the canne, and carry at the same time the left foot pivoting to the side making thus to face 2. The canne on the right shoulder, develop then a third face strike to the left towards 3 and stop the canne on the left shoulder.

These three strikes have only been struck with a single change of facing from 3 to 2.

For the second change of facing, the left foot being on 3, the right on O, make again the double face strike, the first facing 2, the second facing to the right towards 1 always in the same impulse of the canne, carrying swiftly the left foot on 3 making to face 1 and develop a third face strike to the left towards 2 stopping the canne on the left shoulder.

For the third change of face, pivot from the left foot from 3 to 2 facing 4, and make again the indicated strikes.

This development is executed swiftly without marking the pauses which seem indicated by the breakdown of the movements.

## 15th Division

*Development in Three Times on the Four Faces by the Left*

Being in false guard, the left foot on O, the right foot on 1, the canne on the right shoulder (see plate no.35) hit two face strikes, the first to the right towards 3, the second to the left towards 4. In order to make these two strikes, advance the left foot from 1 to 2, making to face 4 turning the head towards 3, making to face thus almost in the same time to 3 and to 4, and without interruption develop a third face strike to the left making to face 4.

Make again in place a double face strike to the right and to the left carrying rapidly the left foot to 3 making to face to 1 and to 2 and it next the third strike to the left facing 1.

Being thus facing 1, repeat again the two face strikes to the right and to the left carrying the left foot on 4 and developing the third face strike towards the left facing 2.

In order to come to face 3, carry the left foot from 4 to 1 repeating the indicated strikes.

This development differs from the previous regarding the step and asks to be much studied.

## 16th Division

*Development in Four Times Doubling Two Face Strikes on the Four Faces by the Right*

Being in true guard, the left foot on 1, the right foot on O, double two face strikes facing 3 and 4, and stop the canne on the left shoulder. Pivot immediately very rapidly on the right foot and carry swiftly the left foot on 4, doubling two face strikes to the left facing 2 and 4.

In order to make the movement again, double two face strikes to the right, stop the canne on the right shoulder, then without pausing, by a sudden pivot movement on the right foot, carry the left foot from 1 to 3 doubling two face strikes always to the right facing 3 and 1.

## 17th Division

*Volté[15] to 4, Five and Six Times in a Straight Line*

### 1st Volté in Four Times to the Right

Being in true guard, the left foot on A, the right foot on 1, develop a first face strike to the right facing B, carrying with a leap[16] the left foot to 3 and by a rapid pivot movement spring from the right foot from 1 to 4 in order to hit a second face strike to the right facing A. Then without changing place[17] by a simple bending[18] of the body, a third strike to the right facing B and a fourth to the left facing A.

Make again immediately the same movements in order to leap successively to points 5, 6, 7, 8.

### 2nd Volté in Four Times to the Left

On these last points 7, 8, that is to say, after three *voltés*, being in false guard, the canne stopped on the left shoulder, making to face A, double a second face strike to the left towards A, passing the right foot from point 8 on 6 and the left foot from 7 on 5, carry immediately two strikes to the left towards B, then a third again to the left towards A, then a fourth to the right towards B, the canne stopped on the right shoulder.

### 3rd Volté at Five and Six Times to the Right

After having leaped as was explained from points A and 1 to 3 and 4, hitting three face strikes to the right, develop immediately without changing place two face strikes to the left, two others to the right, then two others towards the left, counting 1, 2, 3, 4, 5, 6. Stop the canne on the left shoulder, make again the second *volté* movement towards the right by the six face strikes. Execute finally a third *volté* movement, but only then count five strikes, stopping the canne on the right shoulder.

In order to return to the point of departure A, execute, following the same rules, the same movements but towards the left.

---

15. In essence, an about face on the spot
16. *en portant d'un bond*
17. *sans bouger de place*
18. *inflexion*

## 18th Division

### *About-Faces Backwards*

Being in true guard, the right foot on A, the left on 1, but facing A, hit two face strikes to the right leaping backwards from the left foot to point 2, making always to face A, pivot at the same time from the right foot from point 1 to point 3, carrying two other face strikes to the right, making then to face B, rolling the canne swiftly in a circle, and achieve by a leap turning towards the right to face A, the right foot on 5 and the left foot on 6, crossing[19] point 4. Double again four face strikes towards the right. At the first strike, leap backwards from the left foot to point 9, at the second strike carry pivoting the right foot on 8 making to face A, the canne on the right shoulder.

In order to come again to the point of departure, spring forward turning oneself from points 9 and 8 to points 7 and 6, and developing two double head strikes, the canne passing towards the left, making to face B, make then a semi-turn towards A, without changing place, in order to hit a double head strike.

Continue these movements until the point of departure A, in order to arrive making to face B.

It should be remarked that each time that one springs forward by a double head strike, one starts from the left making to face A, the canne on the right shoulder, and that after the two changes of guard effectuated in the movement, one is found facing B. It is for this reason that in order to hit facing A, one makes a semi-turn in place.

## 19th Division

### *Moulinets in the Straight Line*

Being in true guard, first double a face strike carrying the left foot on point 2, then without pausing advance the right foot on 3, falling into true guard and hit a double head strike.

Repeat these movements of the double face strike and double head strike by two changes of guard until point B.

In order to beat a retreat, carry the right foot backwards from 9 to 7 doubling the face strike and carrying the left foot from 8 to 6 hitting a double head strike.

In these movements, hold the right hand lifted backwards in order to make the canne describe very quickly the horizontal circle that it has to follow, the left

---

19. *franchissant*

hand behind on the kidneys, the chest well covered, the right shoulder making to face directly before one, the body slightly inclined towards the left in order to give more momentum to the rotational movement of the canne for the head strike. (See plate no.7)

## 20th Division

### *Moulinets by About-Face Backwards and Forwards*

Being in true guard, double a face strike to the right and carry the left foot on 2, make a *moulinet*, develop immediately a double head strike leaping with the right foot from 1 to 3, with the same momentum, by a rapid turn to the left, the left foot pivoting from 2 to 5. Bring the canne on the right shoulder and hit a second head strike, falling into true guard facing A.

In this position stretch a face strike facing A, pivot carrying the feet from 4 and 5 to 7 and 9, stop the canne on the right shoulder and, in this pivot movement, hit a double head strike, one before, the other behind.

After this double change of guard and facing, make without pausing a double head strike facing B. Hitting this double head strike, carry the right foot from 7 to 9, then pivot advancing the left foot on B, and lengthen a head strike facing A.

Passing through these indicated movements, come again to the point of departure A in true guard.

## 21st Division

### *Triple Moulinets and About-Faces Forward to the Right and to the Left*

Being in false guard, the double face strike made,[20] the left foot advanced to 2, hit, making an about face from points 1 and 2 to points 3 and 4, a double head strike, the first towards B, the second towards A. Immediately these two strikes hit, without stopping the movement of rotation of the canne which must continue to describe a horizontal circle, make a half-turn to the left towards B.

Repeat the movement which was just indicated a second time, then a third time, travelling then to points 9 and B, the left foot on B, the right foot on 9, remain facing A. After having hit the double head strike, bring the canne on the right shoulder and develop four face strikes making an about face by the left; the first strike, carry leaping the left foot from B to 7 and the right foot, passing

---

20. literally: sent, *envoyé*

it behind the left, from 9 to 6, stop the canne on the right shoulder, turn the head towards the left developing four face strikes on this side, leap at the same time by an about-face to the right from points 7 and 6 to points 4 and 3 stretching a face strike to the right in order to bring the canne to the right, make the *moulinet*, then the canne being in movement, by this movement hit a double head strike turning to face B, the right foot passing from point 3 to point 1, and the left from 4 to A, in true guard.

## 22nd Division

### *Development by Six Strikes in Place by the Four Faces*

In order to understand this progression, we reproduce the square diagram with the points already indicated.

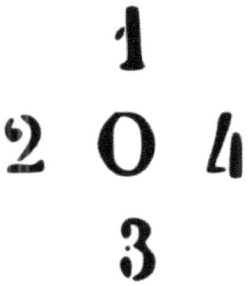

Being in true guard the left foot on 1, the right on O, develop a first face strike facing 3, follow it with a head strike towards the left, by a half-turn to the left pivoting on both feet, the canne passed then towards the left, the hand lifted, inverted the fingers in the air, the little end of the canne directed towards point 1.

Develop then without delay, without pausing, a double head strike, the first towards the right facing 1, the second facing 3, turning rapidly from this side, hit immediately and follow it with a face strike and bring the canne to the right shoulder.

By these movements, one has beaten faces 1 and 3.

In order to beat faces 4 and 2, double the face strike towards the right, pivoting of the left foot on 4, the canne brought in the same time on the right shoulder, develop from the same momentum a double head strike towards 4, hitting the first towards 2, and by a rapid half-turn in place of the body and of the head towards the left, the second towards 4.

For this movement, lifting the hand inverting the fingers in the air, pass the canne the little end of the canne before one.

In order to beat the two other faces, begin by a double face strike towards the right, rapidly pivot towards the left, making a head strike, and follow the series of movements that we have just indicated.

## 23rd Division

*Voltés on the Four Faces with Moulinets and Head Strikes to Fall into True Guard*

Being in true guard in the position marked by the diagram above-mentioned, make a sidestep[21] with the right foot towards the right, lifting the hand towards the left, then develop four face strikes to the right, carrying the left foot forward of the right foot towards the right. Continue the movements of the four face strikes towards the right, make a rapid half-turn leaping from the left foot towards the right, the left foot forward of the right making the canne thus face 4. Stop on the right shoulder, hit a double head strike, the first send to 2, spring rapidly from this side by a half-turn to the left, the left foot finding itself then before the right.

From this point immediately lift the hand backwards, execute the *moulinet* and hit a double head strike, while pivoting on the left foot, the right foot sent forward, the first strike hit facing 4, the second facing 2, and falling into true guard, facing from this side.

Double then two face strikes, the first facing 2, the second facing 4, by a half-turn from this side, and falling into true guard facing 4.

Here is the diagram:

---

21. *écart*. Literally, a burst. In context, sidestep seems more appropriate.

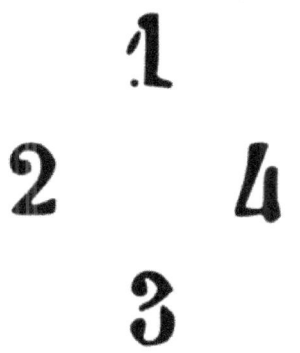

In order to travel through the indicated four points of the diagram, make again the movements that we just demonstrated following the order of their indication.

## 24th Division

*Voltés by Sidestep on the Four Facings, Double Development in Place of the Double Moulinet, and About-Face with Double Head Strike.*

Being in true guard, making to face to point 3, begin by developing a double face strike to the right in order to make immediately a sidestep to the right, *volté*-ing by four face strikes to the right by the same changes of guard as in the 23rd Division.

Arrived at point 2 making to face point 4, by a fourth face strike pivoting, continue the movement lifting the hand backwards and making the *moulinet*, the left foot forward, leap towards 4 by a double head strike, the first facing 4, the second rapidly turning towards 2, finding oneself then facing 2.

From this point make an about-face developing first a face strike facing 2 then, pivoting on both feet in order to look towards the left, hit a double head strike, the first towards 2, the second towards 4. Double next a double face strike springing by two changes of guard towards the right, the first strike made towards 2 and the second towards 4. Without stopping the movement of the canne, lift the hand backwards, the left shoulder making to face at 4, execute the *moulinet* and hit the double head strike, the right foot carried forward, in order to fall into true guard facing 4.

Make again next the entire series of strikes indicated during the journey[22] from point 1 to 4 in order to finish the four facings.

## 25th Division

*Balanced Brisé,[23] Double Development in Place, the First Forwards by Four Face Strikes to the Right, the second by a Double Head Strike in Place with Half to the Left in Place on the Left Foot, Step Forward by Four Face Strikes and Double Head Strike*

Being in true guard on the straight line from A to B, which is to be travelled, place the canne in the position indicated by plate no.32, the right hand on the chest, the little end of the canne a little inclined backwards towards the left, make a double development by the movement indicated nos. 3, 4 and 5 for the first part, all in place, develop next four face strikes towards the right, *volté*-ing forward.

In order to execute this movement, remove the left foot from point A and carry it to point 3 turning towards the right, the right foot passing behind the left foot and going to be placed on 4.

Executing it, make the canne roll horizontally in order to, at the fourth turn, stop it on the right shoulder, making thus to face to point A.

Immediately double two head strikes in place, the first facing A, the second facing B, rapidly turning towards the left.

In this movement, the left foot is removed from point 4 in order to pass in front of the right to point 5, following the movement of the double head strike and making thus to face B.

From this point, being in true guard, spring forward in developing four face strikes turning towards the right, the canne brought to the right shoulder, then make again a leap forward, the right foot carried forward, and send two face strikes, the first towards B, the second making a semi-turn to face A, falling thus into true guard.

In order to return to the point of departure A, take again the series of movements indicated.

---

22. *trajet*
23. *the brisé is a timed vertical strike to the opponent's head from a moulinet interrupting the opponent's preparation to attack.*

## 26th Division

*Balanced Brisé, About-Face in Place with Spring Forward by a Double Head Strike, and Brisé on the Side Pivoting in Place*

Being in true guard, execute the balanced *brisé* and the *volté* – facing in place. After the double head strike, the right foot is found on 4, the left on 3, making to face to A. At the second head strike, then double two face strikes, the right foot remaining in place, the left following the movements of the canne, the body is inclined at each strike either to the left or to the right, the foot following the movements according to whether the strike is made either to the left or to the right.

The balanced *brisé* to the right, the canne brought to the right shoulder, the left foot stopped on 3, facing B, advance the left foot on 5 and the right on 4, and spring forward while pivoting by a double head strike, from points 4 and 5 to points 7 and 8 crossing point 6.

In order to execute this movement, carry the right foot on 7, hitting thus the first head strike, and the left foot on 8, and making a semi-turn and hitting the second head strike facing A.

From this point, make an about-face by two changes of guard, in order to arrive at points 9 and B, making to face A.

Repeat it all in order to finish at point A, facing B.

## 27th Division

*Development in Four Times, Pivoting in Place in order to Make to Face to Two Sides, About-Face to the Right, Double Brisé to the Right and to the Left Pivoting in Place; Spring Forward and About-Face by a Double Head Strike*

Being in true guard, develop two face strikes to the right, and a third strike to the left. At the first strike, hit facing B, carry the left foot from A to 2 and hit the second strike facing A making a half-turn in place and, marking a slight pause, the canne on the right shoulder, hit the third to the left without moving place.

Make again the double *brisé* to the right carrying the right foot on A, and hitting the second strike towards B, then, without moving place, develop a third *brisé* strike towards the left, the canne brought to the left shoulder, *volté* next forward by four face strikes passing the right foot from A on 3, and, turning towards the right, bring this foot from 3 on 4.

From this point, execute the double *brisé* turning on the four faces by a pivot movement on the right foot. Then carry the left foot from 3 to 5, the canne stopped on the right shoulder, spring towards B, hit a double head strike turning the first strike made towards B, the second towards A. Execute next a double about-face turning rapidly towards the left in order to return to point B facing A.

## 28th Division

*Double Balanced Brisé Forward, About-Face in Place, Double Brisé to the Right and to the Left on the Four Faces, About-Face to the Right and to the Left in the Straight Line*

Being in true guard, the right hand on the chest towards the left, the little end of the canne behind, at the first "balanced" carry the left foot to the right heel at point 1. In order to take the right guard, hit immediately a balanced *brisé*, carrying the right foot from 1 to 2, then, at the second "balanced" close again the left foot to the right heel, at point 2, in right guard. (See plate no.32)

Make again a new balanced *brisé* carrying the right foot on 3, hit a *brisé* from the side turning the head towards A. Make a double head strike, front and back. After the second strike, make a *volté* in place pivoting on the left foot, making to face B.

Then double a face strike to the right, carrying the left foot from 2 to 4, and bring the canne to the right shoulder. Make immediately double *brisés* from the side starting to the left. Pivot on the right foot after these double *brisés* on the four facings, and stop the left foot on 5 looking towards B.

Carry immediately the canne to the right shoulder, the right foot on 6, doubling a face strike towards the right, in order to use the same momentum a *volté* in four times on the right by two changes of guard, and arrive thus at point B facing A.

## 29th Division

*Flying Point Strike, Parry in Two Hands, Double Volté by the Left, Horizontal Side Brisé in Three Times on the Four Facings, Pass Forward in Place, Double Head Strike Springing and About-Face in Place*

Being in false guard, double a face strike to the left facing B, carry the right foot forward and grasp the little end of the canne with the left hand in the pose indicated in plate no.36.

Carry the right hand to the chest and the left behind.

From this point hit a flying point strike dropping the right hand, then without releasing the canne from the left hand grasp the handle with the right hand, advancing the left foot and making a parry with two hands. (See plate no.38)

Send then four face strikes flying towards the left, develop the horizontal *brisés* in three times pivoting on the right foot. Stop with the left foot towards B and the canne on the right shoulder, hit a double head strike pivoting in place, executing the pass forward on the four faces in order to spring next by a double head strike towards B finishing, and about-face in place in order to make to face to point A.

Make again the same series of movements in order to come again to the point of departure A making to face B.

## 30th Division

*Double Point Strike in Two Hands, Parry in Two Hands, Double Face Strike Pivoting on the Left Foot, Double Side Brisés Pivoting on the Right Foot and Turning on the Four Facings, About-Face Forward and Moulinet in order to Spring to the Side by a Double Head Strike*

We believe we must reproduce the indicative work of the four facings in order to understand these different movements.

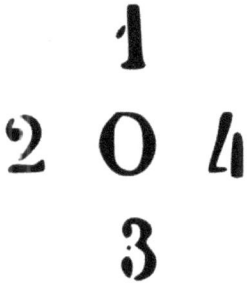

Being in false guard, the canne in two hands, threatening a point strike towards the left (see plate no.41) extending immediately the left arm which is found supported on the chest in order to push again[24] the little end of the canne with the two hands, then without releasing the canne from the left hand in the position of the flying point strike, send it carrying the left foot forward and taking the parry with two hands making to face 4.

---

24. *repousser*

From this position triple a face strike towards the left pivoting on the left foot after having released the canne from the left hand.

Being thus facing 1 the canne on the left shoulder, the left foot behind the right, execute a *volté* towards the right by two changes of face carrying the left foot forward from the right, and take the moulinet movement making thus to face 4.

Spring immediately from point 1 on point 4 by a double head strike, and falling into false guard at the second strike facing 2.

Being placed again immediately in the original[25] position, in false guard, the left hand on the chest, in the position indicated above.

In order to pass by all the points from the diagram, it should be repeated three times the series of previous movements.

---

25. *primitive*

# Post–Face

We are not only teachers of fencing. We do not teach exclusively the handling of the épée, the sabre, the canne. We are also, by a necessary consequence of our teaching, a teacher of exercises which enter more essentially into gymnastics. Here we want to speak of French Boxing.[1]

The observations which we will present in this regard are therefore completely disinterested,[2] truly impartial. They will only be the expression of our conviction, of our experience, our two sole guides in the practice of our profession.

French Boxing, we start by proclaiming it highly, is an exercise of which one knows not well enough [how] to advertise the advantages from the gymnastic point of view, the wholesome point of view.[3] It gives, by the simple play of the limbs without aid of all these machines which one meets in the gymnastic schools, the agility, suppleness, vigour.

After some months of lessons, one is actually surprised by the strength that one has acquired; the arms, the legs have lost their original stiffness, they have suppled, the kidneys for their part have gained in solidity as in elasticity. The man who knows French Boxing is transformed. He becomes supple, light, skilled, more vigorous. He acquired even one exceptional cause of strength, confidence in himself, consequently[4] the self-assurance, solidity in the face of danger.

Here are the actual advantages of which we are happy to note he acquired: he should nonetheless note also that they lose a little of their value if one finds oneself in a struggle with an adversary larger, stronger.

We will agree, it is true, and very readily, that skill, agility, in these circumstances, can substitute[5] for strength, for size. But one must agree also that the length of the arms, of the legs, the solidity of the torso,[6] through the effect of the heaviness of the mass, they present on their side the material advantages which allow not only of having an importance, [but?] a real value.

1. *la boxe française*
2. *désintéressées*
3. *au point de vue salutaire*
4. *par suite*
5. *suppléer à*
6. *l'assiette du corps*

One in vain uses skill, agility, vigour only against a wall, the wall will resist always by its weight alone.

One is therefore brought, by the logic of facts, to recognise that the man smaller, less strong, whatever may be his agility, his skill and even his relative vigour, will be nearly always held in check by a man larger, stronger, however, less skilled, less nimble.

Could this inferiority exist for the man who is a canne carrier and who knows how to handle it?

No. We proclaim it loudly, with all the sincerity of our conviction, with all the power of our experience. No, the man armed with a canne fears not the man larger, stronger than him, even if armed similarly with a canne. We say further, if he knows well to use this defensive arm, he can stand up to[7] three and even four adversaries.

Here, it is not a question of strength, of the length of the members. It is purely and simply a question of self-control,[8] of confidence in oneself, of agility, of suppleness, a question of the handling of the canne.

By our theory, by our practice, by our system of teaching in ten lessons, it is resolved. We do not want to enter into further developments. We will content ourselves to repeat that which we said in our foreword: experience has established the fact of our assertion.

The canne, we say in order to finish, this object of luxury, of fashion, this defensive weapon, so serious, so real, removes from us the danger of carrying a pistol on oneself, from the repulsion of carrying a dagger.

With a pistol, outside of the personal risk which can be exposed by imprudence and neglect[9] can expose, one can kill an adversary that one could otherwise only be put out of harm's way.[10]

With a dagger, moreover, one is not in many circumstances master of the blow struck, and one feels anyway a repugnance instinctive, legitimate, to serve oneself with a weapon which brings with it the odious idea of the ambush.

The canne is, therefore, the only weapon which really fits in a system of personal defence. Only, as [with] the épée, as [with] the sabre, one should learn to handle it.

The handling of the canne is only derived from fencing properly called.

---

7. *tenir tête à*
8. *sang-froid*
9. *oubli*
10. *mettre hors d'état de nuire*

*Figure 1-2: The pad; the student developing a face strike being in true guard.*

*Figure 3: The student developing a face strike, guard on the left or false guard.*

*Figure 4: The student developing a face strike towards the right, extended, the hand in quarte, the thumb above.*

48  La Canne Royale

*Figure 5: The student developing a head strike, extended, the hand in quarte.*

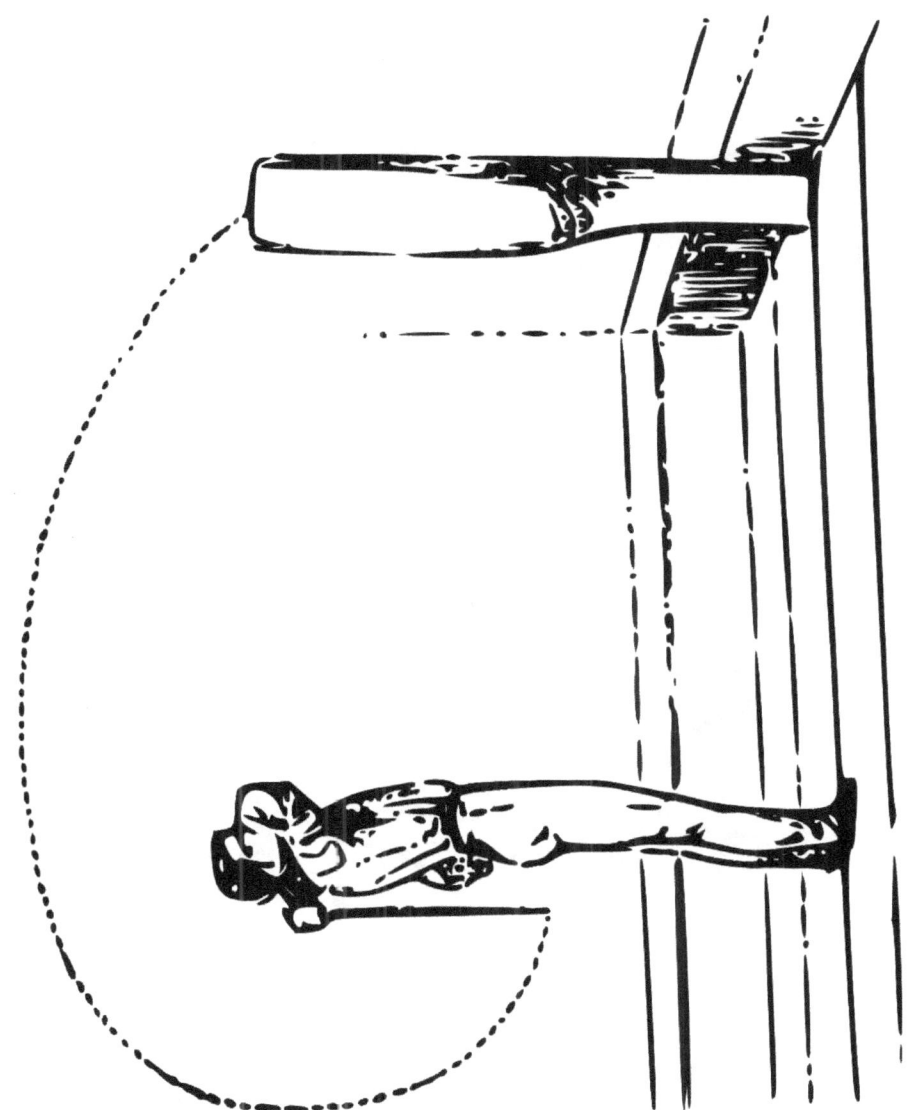

*Figure 6: The student in right guard preparing for a head strike.*

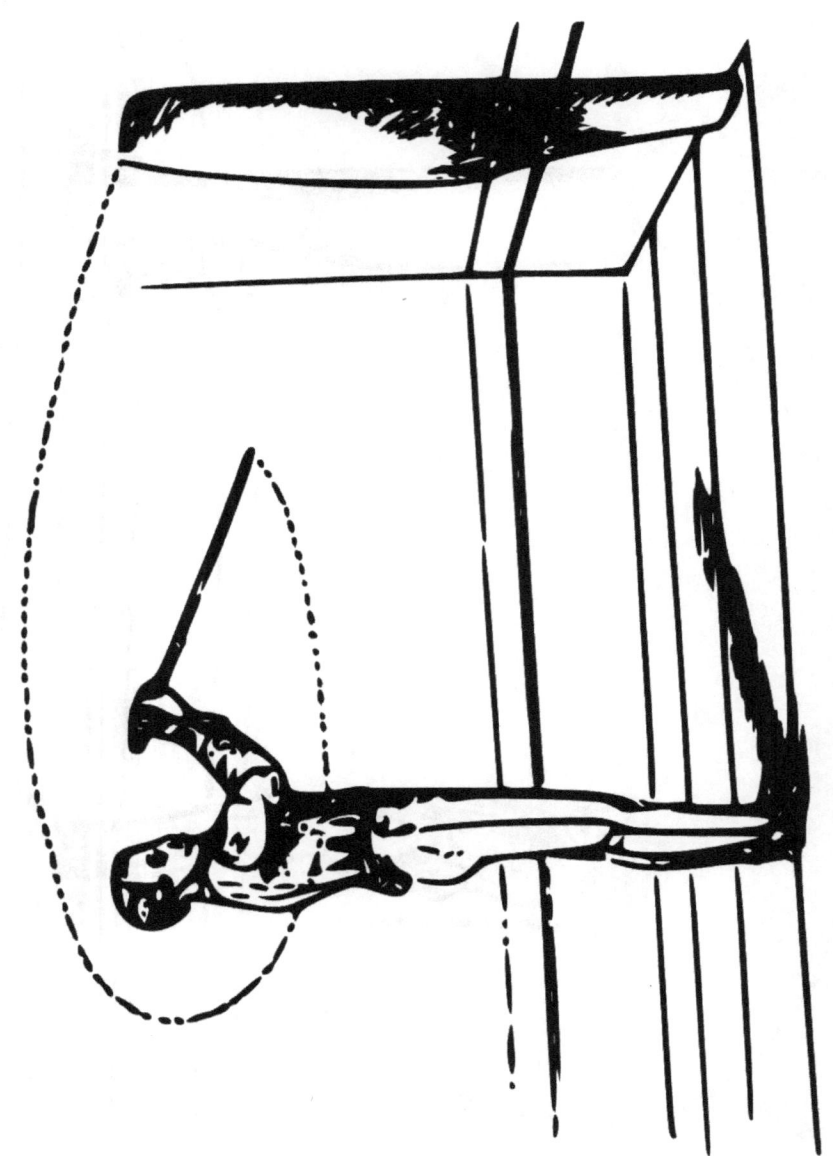

*Figure 7: The student preparing for a head strike passing the canne towards the right, the fingers in the air.*

*Figure 8: The student making a moulinet in order to hit a head strike.*

*Figure 9-10: The student protecting the head, right guard, head strike, extended.*

*Figure 11-12:* Face strike, false guard, the hand in tierce, face parry, the hand in quarte parrying towards the right, right guard.

*Figure 13-14: Preparing a face strike being in false guard, the hand in quarte, and face parry to the left, true guard.*

*Figure 15-16: The point strike finished, followed with a head strike, extended in front of the teacher, in true guard.*

*Figure 17-18: Head parry, the hand inverted in quarte, being in true guard and the head strike extended.*

*Figure 19: Preparing the balanced brisé being in true guard in front of the teacher who takes the low hand parry.*

## 58  La Canne Royale

*Figure 20-21: Kidney strike being extended, kidney parry towards the right being in true guard.*

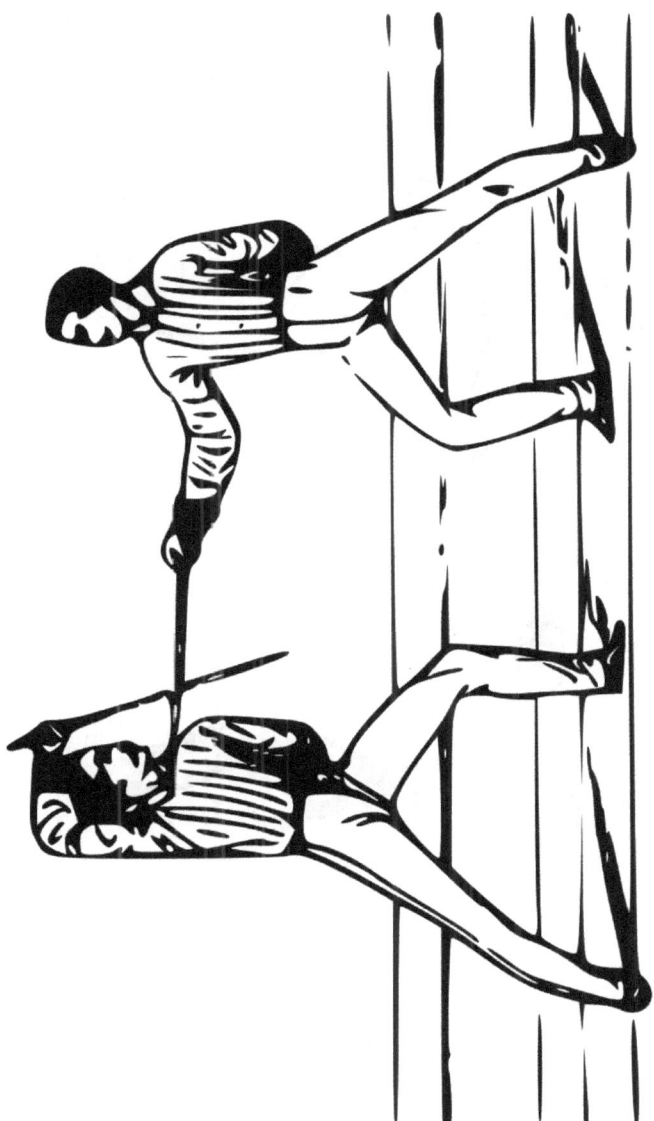

*Figure 22-23: Kidney parry in false guard and the kidney strike*

*Figure 24-25: Leg strike, being extended, avoids with the right leg and the head strike, in false guard.*

*Figure 26-27: Head parry after leg strike, being extended, avoids with the leg and head strike.*

*Figure 28-29: Feint with the simple point strike, being in false guard, the point strike, the parry in true guard.*

*Figure 30-31: Face parry towards the right, being in false guard and the face strike, the hand in tierce in true guard*

# 64 La Canne Royale

*Figure 32: Balanced or breaking of the wrist on the head strike, being in true guard, in front of the teacher.*

*Figure 33: Breaking of the wrist after the "balanced," being in true guard, in front of the teacher.*

*Figure 34: Preparing the development on four faces and the voltés towards the right.*

Figures 67

*Figure 35: Preparing the double voltés to the right and to the left and the voltés towards the left in front of the teacher.*

*Figure 36: Feint a flying point strike in front of the teacher.*

*Figure 37: Flying point strike in front of the teacher.*

*Figure 38: Kidney parry after the flying point strike.*

*Figure 39: Head parry after the flying point strike.*

## 72  La Canne Royale

*Figure 40: The head strike broken backwards after the flying point strike on the head parry.*

*Figure 41: The double point strike with two hands.*

*Figure 42: The teacher placing his student in front of him, in true guard, the hand in quarte.*

# Treatise and Theory of the Canne Royale

by Eugène Hume and J. Renkin

First Edition

Printed by M.-J. Poot and Company, Brussels

1862

Deposited with the French Legation

# Introduction

The desire to be useful to masters and to amateurs is the only motive which guides us in publishing this work.

We are not aware of any treatise of this nature [which] exists and, although ours is very abbreviated, we believe [we] have omitted nothing essential.

For the reader's ease, we have given in one of our chapters the ways of striking[1] together with an explanation of the terms that we employ in the art of the canne. In this manner, we can teach him without being obliged to stop in order to give him a description of each movement.

If, for example, we speak to him of a head strike,[2] he has only to be aware[3] of the chapter which describes it. Our lessons will thus be made without the least interruption and, by consequence, within reach of everyone.

We believe it necessary to inform our readers that before publishing this work, we visited all the principal *salles d'armes* of Paris and Brussels where we had the honour to fence with the best masters and that it is only after having studied their diverse methods that we hazard, in our capacity as fully qualified members[4] of several fencing societies, to bring into the day[5] this treatise, very incomplete without doubt, but for which, seeing our intention, we ask for the greatest leniency.

## Chapter I – The Canne: Its Utility

It is carried in the hand. Its work is not subjected to fixed rules because all strikes are good. This art is truly a game. Its sole aim is to avoid the strikes of the adversary and make the most possible on him without having regard for any part of the body.

Despite that, it is well understood that strikes must be applied according to principles. Thus, it would be committing a great error to suppose the work of the canne to be a confused art. But in comparing it by point and by counterpoint, etc, it is easy to see that the rules to follow are not severe. This will not, however, prevent the young people who engage in this type of exercise of hav-

---

1. *la manière de porter les coups*
2. *un coup de tête*
3. lit: to take knowledge of
4. *membres brevetés*
5. *mettre au jour*

ing, from their start, certain difficulties to overcome. Also, we can only advise them to have great perseverance and soon they will feel the physical benefit of this art which gives to the body a graceful suppleness and corrects all the inherent constitutional faults, so to speak, of childhood.

Thus, we have seen young people bow-legged and bent, be completely straightened[6] by this powerful exercise. We have seen others of a timid and almost craven character earn a reserved boldness and prudent bravery.

We will attempt, by a last example, to prove the numerous benefits of the canne.

You may be attacked by several malefactors armed with clubs and knives. Your cane will suffice to put them all to flight, avoiding the blows that they seek to give you and, in your turn, applying [blows] to them which put them at your mercy.

This is only necessary to induce you to practice such a fine art. The canne is, in its way, the arm of the bourgeois as steel is that of the soldier.

## Chapter 2 – Advice to Masters

We urge those who are engaged[7] in teaching the canne to put in their method the greatest brevity possible without it being obscure. We advise them, above all, of first understanding the character of the student, his strength, and physical qualities. Thus, one should use greater softness with one student than with another, manage those who have late[8] dispositions, pass over certain little faults, while maintaining the necessary strictness[9] in order to not allow them to contract bad habits, having enough patience, if necessary, to make them repeat the same thing a thousand times — in a word, to exercise their strength gradually. Because one particular student will have a disposition much more precocious than another, another will burn with very strong ardour and, in this case, he should master it, because often too much activity becomes more dangerous than slowness.

It is necessary that the master make the student understand that without moderation it is impossible to acquire judgement and presence of mind, two essential things in the art of fencing and especially in the art of the canne. The proof is that it is not astonishing to see a beginner of calm character acquire the

---

6. *redressés*
7. *se livrent*
8. late developing?
9. *sévérité*

greatest strength. For the master, it is thus the moment most favorable for conducting the student to true practice.

We will finish this chapter with a [piece of] final advice. It is well to keep oneself from letting students bout one another before they understand perfectly all the lessons, both in theory and in practice, because it is painful to us to have to say that, with our own eyes, we have seen teachers put immediately all their students to the boot[10] before having given them the least notion of the principles. We aver that he must have very little affection for his art in order to act so lightly.

## Chapter 3 – Advice to Students

There are definitely some things to advise those who want to engage in the art of the canne. We will enumerate the qualities that are necessary in the fencer. The student, therefore, will have only to work in order to acquire them.

He must show the greatest possible moderation, have a modest and assured countenance, listen without disregarding good counsel, reject all smugness,[11] keep his composure,[12] drive away all fear, maintain a firm confidence. Because to intimidate oneself and lose one's steadfastness[13] before the adversary is to run in the face of danger[14] and put obstacles in one's designs. One should not stifle[15] action because, without action, it is not possible to acquire this flexibility of body and this subtlety so necessary in a fencer. Certainly, not.

Thus, we urge strongly the student to teach himself judgement, to penetrate the designs of the opponent and wait with form foot, not to retreat before the strike, to seek to come to the parry and riposte in the same moment. From there comes this speed, this promptness, this quickness and this activity — qualities which are common to good fencers.

To always take the parry is rigorously commanded because seeking to catch the adversary in the moment where he occupies himself with preparing his attack, is to be already hit. Never take advantage[16] from timed strike.[17] Come first to the parry and then, without the least interruption, make a riposte immediately.

10. Idiom? Or, to the bout, to the strike?
11. *fatuité*
12. *son sang-froid*
13. *fermeté*
14. *c'est courir au-devant du danger*
15. *manquer*
16. *ne profitez jamais*
17. *coup de temps* - a single-tempo response

We repeat: the canne is a game once combat has started. It is necessary to be always moving, to retake the guard nimbly and to wait so that the opponent retake it when he is hit.

It happens sometimes that the master does not wait for his student to retake the guard. He parries the blow and he strikes another at him immediately. We urge him who commences practising the canne not to be put off by this method. It is good because it gives a lot of liveliness. But, the teacher can put it into practice only during the five or six first lessons. Continuing it for a long time could harm the student.

One last word to end this chapter.

It is important to take note that the canne is held always between the thumb and the index finger, the other fingers resting half closed.[18] It is necessary to take care to hold it lightly and to leave the greatest play possible. We will even say that it is the secret of the art. [It is] to the student, now, to follow our advice.

## Chapter 4 – Equipment

One chooses a canne of hardwood, a mask furnished inside and out with a large and thick padding of horsehair hiding half the head and the ears completely, the majority of the forehead and part of both cheeks. The middle of the face is protected by an iron grill which must be very narrow.[19] It is necessary that the mask is crossed on the exterior by a strap surrounded by leather in order that one can fix it with ease to the head.

The hand with which you hold the canne must be covered by a padded glove and covered with a sleeve[20] intended to protect the forearm.

Large slippers[21] cannot hurt.

A good *gilet*[22] of leather, well fitting on the chest and all around the arms, is a thing indispensable.

The pants are at the whim of the fencer. However, we have seen masters, and thus students, bout with simple pants of canvas, a mask, glove and a fine shirt.

The thing is not astonishing because, after longer or shorter effort, one easily gets used to the blows and one even prefers to be dressed lightly.

---

18. *à demi fermés*
19. ie: with a fine mesh - *très-étroit*
20. *crespin*
21. *pantoufles*
22. another term for plastron or chest protector

## Chapter 5 – Explanation of Terms

**Botte:** It is a strike made with success. The strike could be simple or compound. It is simple when it is made with a single movement, compound when one or two feints are necessary in order to achieve it.

**Feints:** They are to pretend to make a certain strike and make another. We count two types of feint. The first is that by which one seeks to make the adversary parry on the opposite side to that [on] which one wants to make the strike. The second is practised in the same manner except it is necessary that one makes it with enough speed so that the opponent has not the time to evade the strike that one feints to hit at him.

**Attack:** is to seek to hit the opponent.

*Appel:*[23] is to stamp one or two times the ground with the right foot leaving it in the same place.

**Parry:** is to avoid the opponent's strike. In the canne, it is impossible to give the designation of the parries. The exercise alone must guide you, giving you the means to avoid such or such a strike. All that we can say is that it is good to parry with the means to be able to protect the flanks and the head. Thus, if one seeks to give you a strike to the head, do not raise your hand too high.

**Riposte:** is to attack the opponent immediately after having made the parry.

**Tick of the Canne:**[24] is to riposte immediately after the parry.

**Tick-Tack:**[25] is to riposte after having made a parry to the opponent's riposte.

**Strike for Strike:**[26] is to hit the opponent at the same time that he hits you with a successful strike.

**Passing Strike:**[27] is to aim the canne badly while seeking to make a strike.

**The Four Faces:**[28] In the sixth, seventh and eighth lessons, we re-do the exer-

---
23. To call
24. *tac de la canne*
25. *le tac-au-tac*
26. *le coup pour coup*
27. *coup passé*

cises at each face. We understand by that the four walls of the salle: the wall which is found on your right; 2nd, that which is found behind you; 3rd, that which is found to your left; the point of departure or that which is found before you. In order to make the four faces, we start always from the right.

**Face:** In the first lesson, three faces are indicated. In order to do these, you place yourself first in guard and turn yourself on your heel right, advancing the left foot, in this manner to face to the right, and during these movements, you *mouliner*[29] to the right. Once the facing is made, you cease the face strikes and place the canne on the right shoulder. For the 2nd and 3rd faces, turn yourself again to the right, as with the first time.

**The Wall:** the wall is a preparatory exercise before the assault. It is composed of the salute.

**Assault:**[30] is real combat between two opponents.

## Chapter 6

### First Position

The body, turned a little towards the left, must be plumb on the hips, the head high, the heel of the right foot against the ankle of the left foot, the feet placed squarely, the right hand holding the canne which rests on the ground, the left arm hanging along the left thigh, the left hand open, the palm outside and the little finger lying along the seam of the pants. (Fig.1)

### Second Position

In order to pass from the first position to the second, we proceed in the following manner. Give a strike to the head before you and immediately bring back the canne to the left shoulder, the right arm folded on the chest. In making this movement, one should place the left hand at the bottom of the back, well removing the arm, carrying the right foot forward a little distance from the left foot equal to the length between the ankle of the foot and the point of the knee. The legs[31] should be straight.

---

28. Compare with Larribeau's four faces. Larribeau starts with 1 directly in front and proceeds anti-clockwise. Humé starts with 1 on the right and proceeds clockwise.

29. The term is not explained but may be deduced from the description of the strikes and relevant lessons. It is a term familiar to fencers.

30. or bout

If instead of having the right foot forward, you have the left foot, give this last position the name of left guard.

The guard can be changed in one of three manners. 1st, by a step[32] in place, 2nd retreating,[33] 3rd, advancing.

It is to be noted that during the lessons, the left hand is not placed behind the back but at the bottom of the throat. By this means, the student avoids certain strikes which he could very well give himself.

## Chapter 7 – Designation of the Strikes

**Face strikes:**[34] Face strikes are those which are given most often in the canne. In order to apply them, the canne should describe one or several circles around the head and target[35] the opponent's face.

Needless to say, face strikes must always be given from the side where one is turned.

**Head Strikes:**[36] Head strikes are applied by making the canne describe one or several circles, be it on one side or be it on both sides of the body.

**Cuts**[37] **/ Flank Strikes:** strikes given hitting the two flanks with the canne.

The cuts are something other than flank strikes with the difference being[38] that, instead of beating one's own flanks,[39] one aims in the assault at those of the opponent while lifting the right elbow a little in order to, at need, come immediately to parry the head strike.

**Stop Strike:**[40] is to plunge the end of the canne which touches ground into the opponent's chest while holding the arm extended. By this means, he cannot approach you. This strike is forbidden. It is even bad grace to pretend to give it.

---

31. *jarrets* - literally, the hamstrings or the back of the knee depending on context
32. *un saut* - strictly speaking this means a leap or a bound but in context a lively step makes better sense.
33. *en rompant*. Not simple to translate although there is a phrase *rompre la semelle* which means to step backwards or withdraw the foot.
34. *coups de figure*
35. *ajuster*
36. *coups de tête*
37. *les coupés*
38. *avec dette difference qu'*
39. *se battre les flancs* is an idiomatic expression for "making a great effort of willpower"
40. *coup d'arrêt*

**Strikes to the Parts**[41] You make a backwards *moulinet* with the canne, and lift it a little while plunging it with force into the opponent's "parts."[42] This strike is banned like the previous [one].

**Leg Strikes:**[43] These strikes are made hitting, either with arms folded or arms straight, the opponent's hamstrings.

**Ankle Strikes:**[44] Ankle strikes are given like leg strikes the only difference that instead of trying to reach the hamstrings one aims to make this strike on the ankles.

**Point Strike:**[45] It is a very cruel strike. In order to apply it, one should throw the canne backwards along the right arm and hit the opponent's face with the end that one holds in the hand.

This strike is given when one is constricted.[46] We urge using it often. Thanks to the mask, it cannot injure. It can get rid of[47] a malefactor promptly who ordinarily only attacks to grab his loot.[48] (Fig.4)

**Arm Strikes, Stomach Strikes, Chest Strikes**[49] are given similarly. We believe it needless dwell at length on the strikes to give. It suffices us to say that one can hit one's opponent everywhere where one finds a vulnerable place.

---

41. *coup de parties*
42. a euphemism for the testicles
43. *coups de jarrets*
44. *coups de cheville*
45. *coup de bout*
46. *lorsqu'on est serré*
47. *débarrasser*
48. *en fondant son butin*
49. *coups de bras, de ventre, de poitrine*

# The Assault – The Bout – The Manner to Comport Oneself

## Chapter 8

Before starting the bout, one fences graciously the wall, which is followed ordinarily with a crowning salute, after which each puts on his mask. The eldest fencer[1] begins the attack. If by accident your opponent's canne falls, it is your duty to recover it and present it to him with politeness.

It ill becomes you to claim to have hit your opponent, above all when he denies the strike. It equally demonstrates a lack of education[2] to deny a strike received or become angry after having been hit. If, after a certain number of strikes, you throw three [strikes] and only on the third you touch your opponent, it is civil to invite your opponent to throw a final strike, which we call the beauty,[3] and which we usually allow to hit.

We believe it needless to expand further on the manner of comporting oneself in the bout.

The student will know that he should use politeness not only with the opponent but also with the public.

For all the physical qualities required, we refer our readers to the chapter **Advice for Students**.

## Chapter 9 – First Lesson

*En garde*.[4] Three faces. Four cuts. On the fourth cut, one should have the canne on the right flank. One face strike to the left, one to the right. In giving the face strike to the left, stretch the right leg[5] and bend the left knee. In giving the face strike to the right, bend the right knee and stretch the left leg. Again two faces. Four cuts. One face strike to the left. One face strike to the right. After these two faces, you have the left foot in front. Come again into guard through a head strike to the left, a head strike to the right. It is with the head strike to the

---

1. *tireur le plus ancien*
2. with an obvious connotation of education to social appropriateness
3. *la belle*
4. Untranslated because the meaning is obvious to a fencer and the translation is unnecessarily lengthy
5. *jarret*

right that guard is retaken carrying the right foot forward. Immediately, change guard by a spring[6] in place, giving face strikes to the right. Having changed guard, you have again the left foot in front, retake guard by a head strike to the left and one to the right.

## Chapter 10 – Second Lesson

*En garde*. Step to the right, first face. After this step, you have the left foot forward. Change guard through a second step, always remaining on the same face. Then, make the second face. Change guard two times with two steps. Next, the third face where you make again two steps. Make a last step to the right to arrive at the fourth face, that of the point of departure. At this last, instead of changing guard two times and having the left foot in front, come again simply into guard through one head strike to the left, one head strike to the right. Change guard with a step and take it again with one head strike to the left, one to the right.

It is useful to recall that during these two steps to change face, one should always give face strikes, changing their direction with each step.

## Chapter 11 – Third Lesson

*En garde*. Make three steps forward,[7] stepping lightly and advancing: for the first step, the right foot; for the second, the left foot; for the third, the right foot.

While making these three small steps, give face strikes changing their direction on each step.

Once these three steps are made, turn around completely, facing the rear, making a step to the left by crossing the legs. Make the three steps again. After the third step, repeat the step by crossing the legs. Change guard by stepping and come again into guard by one face strike to the left, one to the right.

## Chapter 12 – Fourth Lesson

*En garde*. Advance the upper body[8] forward and double the length[9] of the guard. Next, throw yourself forward as far as possible while giving face strikes and settle again[10] on the right foot, the left foot forward, facing to the right. Give four

---

6. *sauter*
7. *devant vous*
8. *le haut du corps*
9. *mesure*
10. *retombez*

cuts: one face strike to the left, one face strike to the right. Retake guard by one head strike to the left, one head strike to the right. Next, change guard with a step and retake it by one head strike to the left, one to the right.

## Chapter 13 – *Volté*

*En garde.* Carry the right foot behind turning to the right on the point of the left foot.[11] Turn a second time, carrying the left foot behind and turning on the point of the right foot. Put back[12] the right foot behind, in a manner to be in guard [with] the left foot forward, making *moulinets* to the right.

Next, the *demi-volte*[13] to the left in front — Carry the right foot forward, turning lightly on the point of the left foot. Turn on the point of the right foot carrying the left foot behind, in the manner to face backwards and the right foot in front, *moulinet* to the left.

Afterwards, the *demi-vclte* behind to the right — In order to turn again to face the front,[14] turn on the point of the right foot and carry the left foot in front. Turn on the point of the left foot carrying the right foot behind making to face backwards. Come again into guard by two head strikes. Change guard by stepping and retake it by a head strike to the left and one to the right.

## Chapter 14 – Fifth Lesson

*En garde.* The same step as in the fourth lesson. Once the step is made, give four cuts: a face strike to the left, a face strike to the right. Repeat this exercise at each facing and even at the fourth. End the lesson with a complete *volte*,[15] a *demi-volte* to the left and a *demi-vclte* to the right.

The change of facing in this lesson is made stepping to the right through the face strikes, the feet parallel.

## Chapter 15 – Sixth Lesson

*En garde.* While giving face strikes, turn to the right on the left heel and place the right foot behind, the middle of the right foot opposite the left heel. Come again into guard through a head strike to the left, one to the right. At a second head strike to the right, leave the right arm raised, the hand before the left

---

11. ie: on the ball of the foot
12. *reportez*
13. half-pivot
14. *de manière à revenir face en tête*
15. full pivot?

shoulder, the point of the canne inclined to the right. In this position, make two *appels* with the foot and, immediately after the second, give an ankle strike. Repeat this exercise at each face, taking care to turn to the right on the left heel each time that you change facing.

Once the exercise of the fourth face is finished, we advise, as this lesson could be applied the wall, having them follow with a crowning salute.

The crowning salute is made in making the canne describe a complete circle above the head from right to left and from left to right. It is obvious that one should incline the head in order to salute spectators. It is the duty of the public to respond to this salute.

## Chapter 16 – Seventh Lesson

*En garde.* Make a *volté* to the four faces, the feet on the same line.[16] At each face, make three head strikes to the right and three strikes to the parts.[17] Take note that these head strikes and these strikes to the parts are given from the side which you will be facing according to that [ie: the side] where you find yourself. Immediately after, make a knee strike but, this time, in front of you. At the fourth face, come again into guard through one head strike to the left, one to the right. Change guard by stepping and come again into guard with one head strike to the left, one to the right.

At the fourth face, you can similarly end the lesson by a complete *volte*, the *demi-volte* to the left and the *demi-volte* to the right.

There are teachers who execute the *volté* at the end of each lesson. Their method is good because it gives a lot of liveliness, agility, and suppleness.

## Chapter 17 – Eighth Lesson

*En garde. Volte* to the four faces. At each face, drop to the ground with a point strike.[18] After that, make a step backwards, always in the same position, that is to say, keeping the right foot forward and the left behind. While making this step, give a flank strike. Next, without interruption, step a second time backwards but, this time, gather the feet on the same line and give a knee strike.

At the fourth face, that of the point of departure, finish with a *volté*.

---

16. *les pieds sur une même ligne*
17. Once again, the euphemism.
18. Presumably the canne rather than the body

## Conclusion

Our task is fulfilled. We repeat that we have not made the claim of offering to our readers a complete treatise on the Canne Royale but only a summary whose aim is to give the more or less fixed rules in an art so ancient but nonetheless so appreciated in our day.

If one deigns to criticise us, we ask that one does so in good faith.[19] But if one wants to profit from our lessons, it would be our greatest recompense because we would have achieved the goal that we proposed in publishing this little treatise.

---

19. *loyalement*

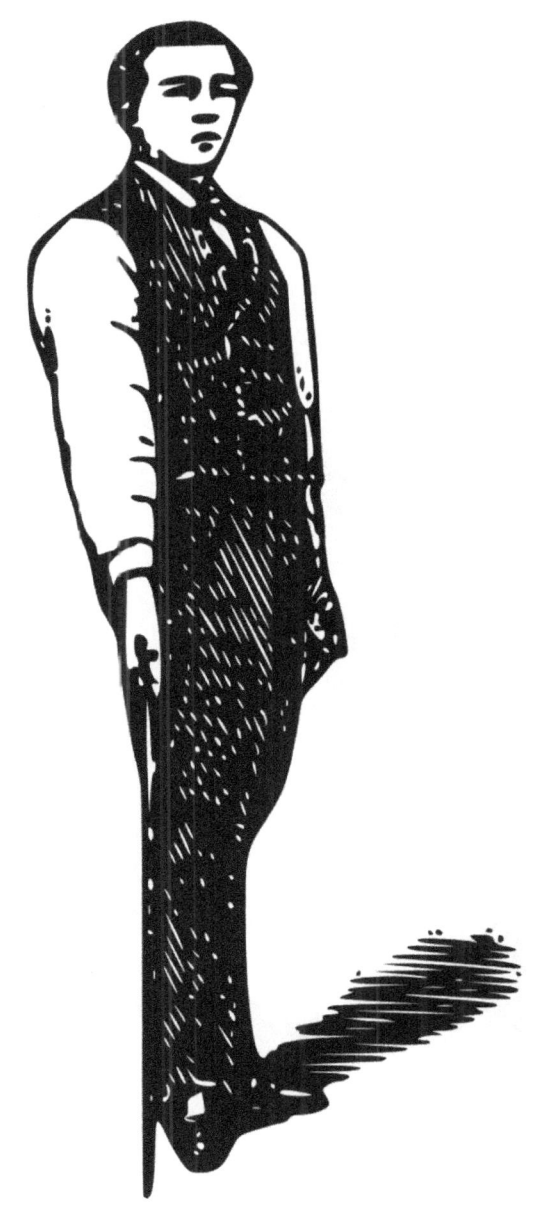

*Figure No 1*

Figure No. 2

*Figure No. 3*

*Figure No. 4*

www.ingramcontent.com/pod-product-compliance
Lightning Source LLC
Chambersburg PA
CBHW020744100426
42735CB00037B/541